The Merry Christmas Activity B❄❄k

Jane Bull

TED SMART

LONDON, NEW YORK, MUNICH,
MELBOURNE, and DELHI

DESIGN • Jane Bull
EDITOR • Penelope Arlon
PHOTOGRAPHY • Andy Crawford
DESIGNER • Sadie Thomas

PUBLISHING MANAGER • Sue Leonard
MANAGING ART EDITOR • Clare Shedden
PRODUCTION • Alison Lenane
DTP DESIGNER • Almudena Díaz

For Grandad
Freddie

First published in Great Britain in 2005 by
Dorling Kindersley Limited
80 Strand, London WC2R 0RL

A Penguin Company

2 4 6 8 10 9 7 5 3 1

This edition produced for The Book People Ltd,
Hall Wood Avenue, Haydock, St Helens WA11 9UL

A CIP catalogue record for this book
is available from the British Library

ISBN: 1-4053-1379-X

Colour reproduction by
GRB Editrice S.r.l., Verona, Italy
Printed and bound in Italy by L.E.G.O.

Have some frosty, festive fun

Make a merry Christmas . . .

Sprinkle sparkly greetings . . .

. . . and cook up some gifts

Glittery greetings

Pour on the glitter and send a Christmas card with added sparkle to your special friends.

Get out your glitter

Collect up all the sparkly
things you can find:

Glitter • Glitter glue pens

Sequins • Wobbly eyes • Stickers

Gift ribbons • Tinsel

You'll also need thin card, a paintbrush,
and some PVA glue.

Conjure up a glitter card

Paint brush

PVA glue

Paint your design with glue.

Fold a piece of thin card in half.

Sprinkle on the glitter.

Put down a sheet of newspaper to catch the glitter.

Shake it off.

Finish your card with extra decoration such as stickers or paint.

Don't waste any!

Fold the newspaper in half.

Pour the glitter back.

Cookie cutter shapes

Any shape cutter will work.

PVA glue

Dip a cutter in glue, press it on the paper, then cover it with glitter.

Special gifts

Wrap and tag

Dip it, print it, wrap it, tag it!
It's great to give gifts but
even better to give them
wrapped in home-made
paper complete with
matching tags.

How to print....

Clear a space, you are now going to do some big printing! Find some plain paper that is big enough to wrap presents in – a roll of brown paper is good – and get printing. Remember to do an extra stencil that you can cut out and turn into a matching tag.

Shooting star stencils

Draw a star on a piece of paper.

Cut out the star.

Place the stencil on your wrapping paper. Dip the sponge into some paint and dab it over the stencil.

Frosty the potato man

Cut a potato in half, dab it in the paint, and press the potato onto the paper. Repeat for the body shape.

Take the stencil off carefully – you don't want the paint to smudge.

You will need:

- Sheets of plain paper
- Sponges
- Odds and ends to print with
- Acrylic paint
- Card for the stencils
- Pen and scissors
- Ribbon or string to attach the tag

Spongy festive forest

Draw your shape on a sponge.

Cut it out.

Glue the sponge onto a piece of card.

Now print your trees onto the wrapping paper and decorate them with red and gold paint.

Pen-top printing

Pen tops make pretty patterns.

Try using the eraser at the end of your pencil.

Use the base of your pen to make a big circle.

Camouflage kit

Print with a scrunched-up plastic bag to make it look like camouflage.

Snowy bunting

Deck your walls
with flurries of snowflakes and
streamers of happy snowmen.

13

How to make snowy bunting

The trick with this bunting is to take a piece of string, then thread your decorations onto it with a straw between each one to separate them. Try these simple ideas.

OLD GREETINGS CARDS

.... Take some old cards and cut them into shapes.

STRAWS

Punch a hole in the paper snow.

STRING

Paper snow

Turn to page 47 for instructions on how to make snowflakes, and string them up for a flurry of festive fun.

SINGLE HOLE PUNCH

LOTS OF PAPER SNOW SHAPES

Paper plate flakes

Now make colourful snowflakes and attach them to paper plates, or turn the plates into cheeky snowmen.

HOLE PUNCH

SCISSORS

GLUE STICK

STRAWS

PAPER

.... Cut the snowman's face out of paper or card and glue it on.

STRING

PAPER PLATES

PAPER SNOW

Glue the paper snow onto the plates.

14

Snowy greetings

Don't throw them out! Last year's greetings cards make instant colourful decorations. Cut the cards into shapes, punch a hole in them, and string them up with straws between each to separate them.

Thread the snowflakes on the string with straws between them.

STRAWS

STRING

Punch holes in the plates.

Thread string through the straws and the holes in the plates.

Remember to knot the ends so everything stays on.

15

Baubles,

...stars, and 3D trees

Make them small to hang on a tree

or huge to hang from the ceiling,

but whatever you do, hang them up!

3D trees

For a 3D look slot two shapes together. Try two circles as well to give a bauble effect.

1. Cut two tree shapes exactly the same.

Cut a slot in one tree from the top to halfway down.

2. Now cut a slot in the other tree.

Cut up from base to halfway up.

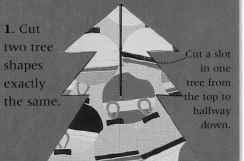

3. Slide one shape onto the other.

4. Stand your tree up, or stick on some thread and hang on the tree.

Paper baubles

If you use old, recycled Christmas cards, all the decorations will be completely different. You could also use your home-made printed paper.

Little or large

String me up and hang me up

17

How to make baubles and stars

For baubles you will need

Old greetings cards • Thick paper • Ruler • Pen • Scissors •
Hole punch • Paper fasteners • Thread

RE-USE OLD
GREETINGS CARDS

Paper baubles

RULER

PENCIL

SCISSORS

1 Cut the card into strips

SINGLE HOLE
PUNCH

Punch the holes
at the bottom
and the top.

2 Punch holes

Tie thread around
the paper fastener
to hang it up.

Clip
the strips
together at the
bottom and the top.

PAPER FASTENER

3 Clip together

4 Fan out the strips to form a ball

18

Super stars

You will need:
Paper • Pen • Scissors • Thread • Tape

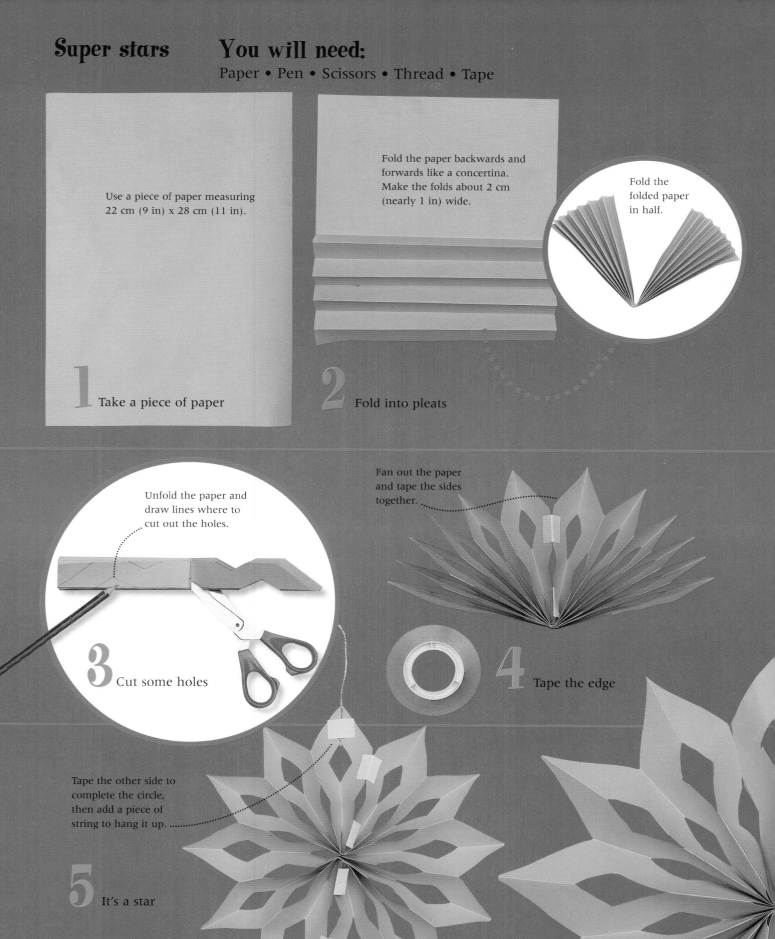

Use a piece of paper measuring 22 cm (9 in) x 28 cm (11 in).

1 Take a piece of paper

Fold the paper backwards and forwards like a concertina. Make the folds about 2 cm (nearly 1 in) wide.

Fold the folded paper in half.

2 Fold into pleats

Unfold the paper and draw lines where to cut out the holes.

3 Cut some holes

Fan out the paper and tape the sides together.

4 Tape the edge

Tape the other side to complete the circle, then add a piece of string to hang it up.

5 It's a star

Christmas night

Hush now, all is quiet.

Light your lanterns and watch them twinkle in the dark to welcome festive friends.

Four decorative designs

When the candle burns, it can reveal a host of angels, colourful spots, stained-glass shapes, or a starlit skyscape. All you need is a jam jar and tissue paper.

Alternatively glue tissue paper circles onto your tracing paper.

3

Tissue paper

Cut out some blue tissue paper the same size as the tracing paper, draw on stars, and cut them out.

2

Cut out a landscape from coloured paper and glue it to the tracing paper.

4

Glue the blue paper to the back of the tracing paper.

Festive forest

1

Cut some tracing paper to fit around a jar.

5

Wrap the sheet around the jar.

Tape in position.

Shining star jar

1 Cut a piece of paper the height of the jar and long enough to fit around it.

2 Snip a zigzag along the top and draw and cut a pattern out of the middle.

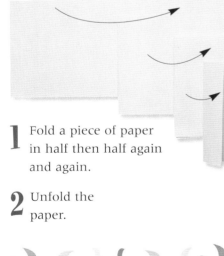

3 Glue a different-coloured piece of tissue paper to the back of the design and wrap the paper around the jar.

Glowing angels

Draw a design on the folded paper, and cut it out.

1 Fold a piece of paper in half then half again and again.

2 Unfold the paper.

3 Make the paper into a crown shape and tape the ends together. Slip it over a large jar.

This design slips over a jar – it's not attached like the others.

23

Festive windows

Day and night give your room a Christmassy glow
with these tissue paper windows

1

SCISSORS

PENCIL

Draw your picture on a sheet of
dark-coloured card, and cut out
some shapes.

2

Glue pieces
of tissue to
the back of
the picture.

GLUE
STICK

COLOURED
TISSUE PAPER

3 Turn your picture
back over.

Now stick your silhouette
in the window and let
it shine out!

Clever cut-outs

Instead of a picture, try cutting out a snowflake from folded paper. Turn to page 47 to find out how to make one.

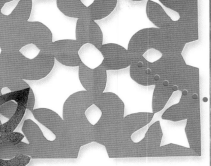

A flurry of snowflake windows.

Winter woolies

Soft and squashy felt decorations hang around with fuzzy pompoms.

How to stitch some woolies

Collect together colourful felts and threads.

Cut out two shapes, sew them up using blanket stitch, stuff them with something soft, and decorate with sparkly sequins. Turn to page 46 to make pompoms.

NEEDLE THREADER

GOLD OR SILVER THREAD

SEQUINS AND RIBBONS FOR DECORATION

LOTS OF DIFFERENT COLOURED FELT

PVA GLUE

PINS

Needles and pins

You will need:
• embroidery needles – use a needle threader to help you thread a needle
• Glue
• Stuffing

COLOURED THREAD

SOFT TOY STUFFING

SCISSORS

Cutting shapes

Turn to page 48 to find the shape templates.

Cover the page with a piece of tracing paper.

Trace over the shapes with a pencil.

Glue a heart to the triangle shape.

Angels and fairies

Cut out, stitch, and stuff

Pin your template onto a piece of folded felt and cut it out.

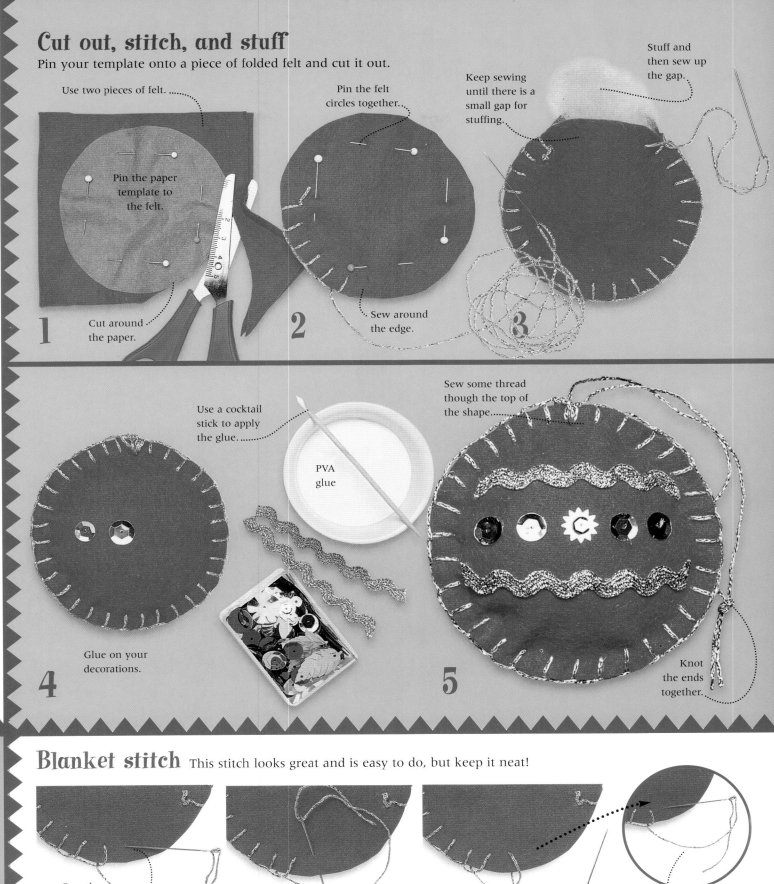

Use two pieces of felt. .....

Pin the paper template to the felt.

Cut around the paper.

1

Pin the felt circles together. .....

Sew around the edge.

2

Keep sewing until there is a small gap for stuffing.

Stuff and then sew up the gap.

3

Use a cocktail stick to apply the glue. ......

PVA glue

Glue on your decorations.

4

Sew some thread though the top of the shape. ....

Knot the ends together.

5

Blanket stitch   This stitch looks great and is easy to do, but keep it neat!

Pass the needle through the felt. .....

1

Bring the needle through and under the thread. ....

2

Pull the needle through. ....

3

That's made a stitch

Ready to start a new stitch? Repeat steps 1, 2, 3.

Christmas scents

Sweet and spicy mixes of cinnamon and cloves with the fruity aroma of orange fills the air. Pomanders and pot pourri – perfect to give as presents.

Making scents

Rich, spicy smells are all around at Christmas time, so why not collect them up and bottle them.

Pour in the ingredients

Mix up a pot of scents

To make pot pourri, spoon spices, such as ground nutmeg and mixed spice, into a jar. Then add cinnamon sticks, nutmegs, cloves, etc. to fill it. Turn the jar over to mix it up and keep it in a cool, dry place. Keep turning it once a day for four weeks.

Place on the lid.

Turn the jar each day.

Keep turning for weeks.

CINNAMON STICKS

NUTMEGS

ALLSPICE BERRIES

ORRIS ROOT

MIXED SPICE

STAR ANISE

Clove-studded oranges

These scented fruit are called pomanders. Oranges work best but you could try other citrus fruits as well. The jewelled pomander will last only a few days but the clove-studded orange will last for much longer.

Wrap some tape around the middle of the orange.

Push the cloves in until the orange is covered.

You will need

PAPER BAG

RIBBON

CLOVES

KUMQUATS

LIME

LEMON

ORRIS ROOT

ORANGE

TANGERINE

MASKING TAPE

GROUND NUTMEG

GROUND CINNAMON

CINNAMON STICKS

FIR CONES

WHOLE CLOVES

After about six weeks your pot pourri will be ready.

POT POURRI • Because the ingredients are dry it will last for ever, but the scent will fade after a few months.

POMANDERS • As the orange dries out it will shrink and only the cloves will show. It will smell nice for weeks.

ORRIS ROOT • You can buy this at health shops and pharmacies. It's used to help preserve the sweet smells.

Glass-headed pins and sequins.

Jewelled pomander

Mix up the pins and the cloves for a colourful, jewelled look.

Put the orris root into a bowl.

Wrap the orange in a paper bag.

Remove the tape and tie it up with a ribbon.

Roll the orange around until it is coated.

Tape up the top.

Leave in a warm dry place for six weeks.

33

Sugar and spice

Yum Yum

Spicy biscuits
With a hint of orange, dipped in sweet icing.

35

Mix up some spice

Stir up the spice - these delicious biscuits can be served up straight away or can be stored in an airtight tin for a few weeks.

ASK AN ADULT to help with the oven.

Set the oven to 190°C/375°F/Gas mark 5

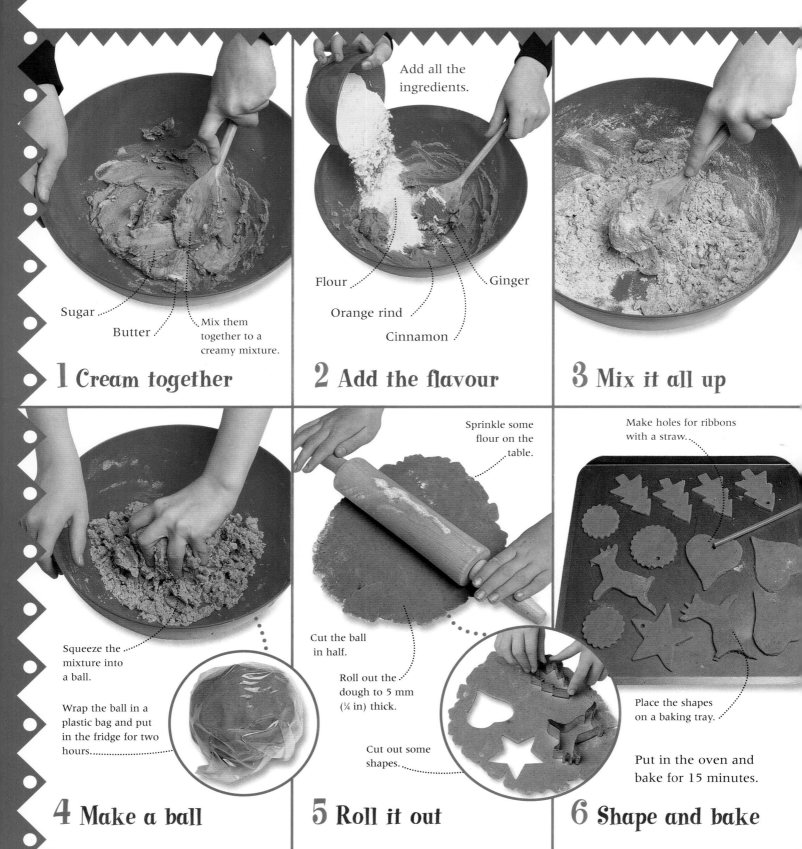

1 Cream together

Sugar

Butter

Mix them together to a creamy mixture.

2 Add the flavour

Add all the ingredients.

Flour

Orange rind

Cinnamon

Ginger

3 Mix it all up

4 Make a ball

Squeeze the mixture into a ball.

Wrap the ball in a plastic bag and put in the fridge for two hours.

5 Roll it out

Sprinkle some flour on the table.

Cut the ball in half.

Roll out the dough to 5 mm (¼ in) thick.

Cut out some shapes.

6 Shape and bake

Make holes for ribbons with a straw.

Place the shapes on a baking tray.

Put in the oven and bake for 15 minutes.

You will need:

170 G (6OZ) BUTTER   85 G (3OZ) BROWN SUGAR   200 G (7OZ) FLOUR   2 TEASPOONS GINGER   2 TEASPOONS CINNAMON   GRATED ORANGE RIND

7 Now decorate

Remove them from the oven and
put them on a rack to cool.

Sugar and water
icing

When the biscuits are cold,
decorate them with icing. Mix
3 tablespoons of icing sugar and
3 teaspoons of water. Decorate
with silver balls, or any other
tasty decorations that you fancy.

Spoon on
the icing
and smooth
it out.

Make a snowman biscuit

Cookie
cutters

Cut two circles.   Join together.   Decorate

Secret snowman

Surprise surprise! What's Frosty hiding under his hat?

Secret snowballs

They're not just a pretty decoration to hang on the tree, but a secret stash of goodies. Give one to a friend and fill it with gifts.

Pull your snowball apart...

...and let the goodies roll out

Off with his hat!
Look what's inside

Make a paper pot

PVA GLUE

BALLOONS

TORN-UP NEWSPAPER

To stop the paper sticking to the balloon, spread vaseline over it.

1
Cover the balloon with PVA glue.

2
Spread pieces of newspaper over the balloon, leaving the bottom uncovered.

3
Repeat steps 1 and 2 six more times. Finish with a layer of PVA glue.

4
Leave it to dry for a day or two.

Use a pot to support it.

Pop!

When it's hard and dry, pop the balloon.

Make a secret snowman

You will need to start with two pots the same size. That means you will have to blow up your balloons to match. One will be for the hat and the other for the head.

2

HAT   **HEAD**

Trim them down

1

The dotted lines show where to trim them down.

First make two pots

Paint and PVA

Mix equal amounts of paint with PVA glue. This gives a nice sheen when it has dried and makes the pot stronger.

FOLD ALONG DOTTED LINES

Nose template
Trace this nose shape and cut it out of card.

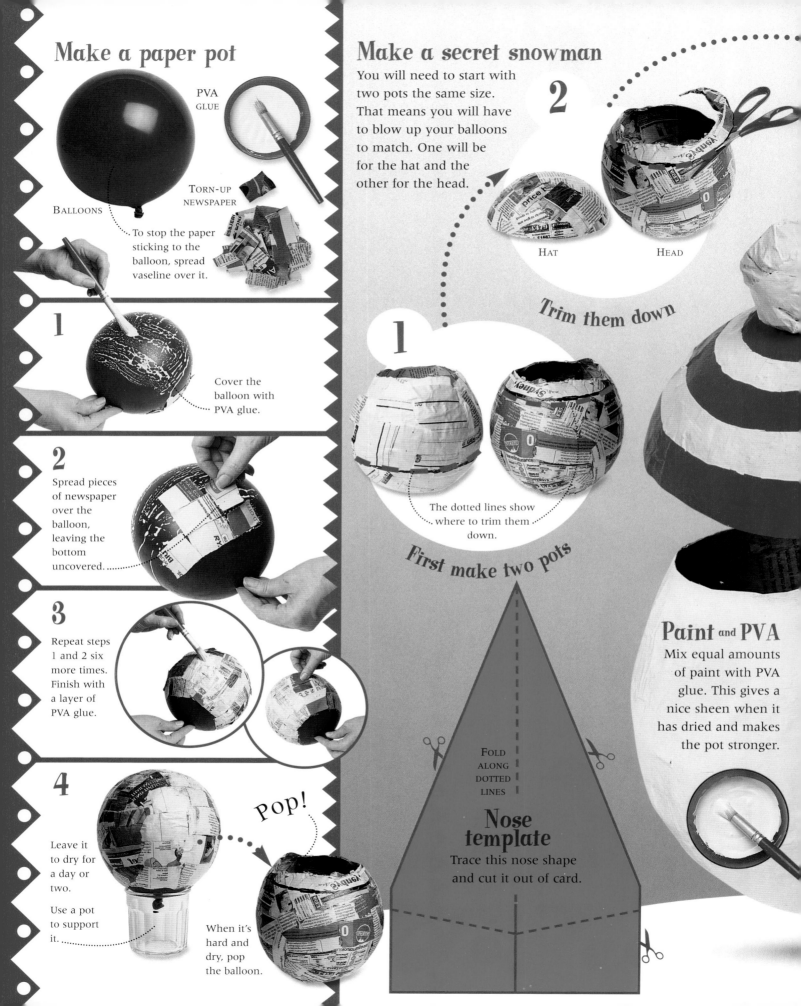

3

MASKING TAPE

Wrap it in masking tape.

Use a strong glue to fix it in place...

Scrunch up some paper into a ball.

Make a bobble

4

Stick on a folded card nose with strong glue.

Paste some pieces of paper over the joins.

Add a nose

5

Paint them with white paint mixed with PVA glue.

Leave them to dry.

Paint them all white

6

Mix the paints with PVA glue.

Give him a face

Make a bauble

Make two pots and this time blow up two smaller balloons to the same size.

1 Make two small pots.

2 Trim them down.

Cover with white paint.

BASE POT   POT LID

3 **Ask an adult** to make a small hole in the bottom of each pot.

4 Decorate the pots with paint and glitter.

5 Take a piece of ribbon 60 cm (22 in) long and tie the two ends together.

Pass the ribbon up through the hole in the large pot.

Push the ribbon through the hole in the lid and now you can hang it up.

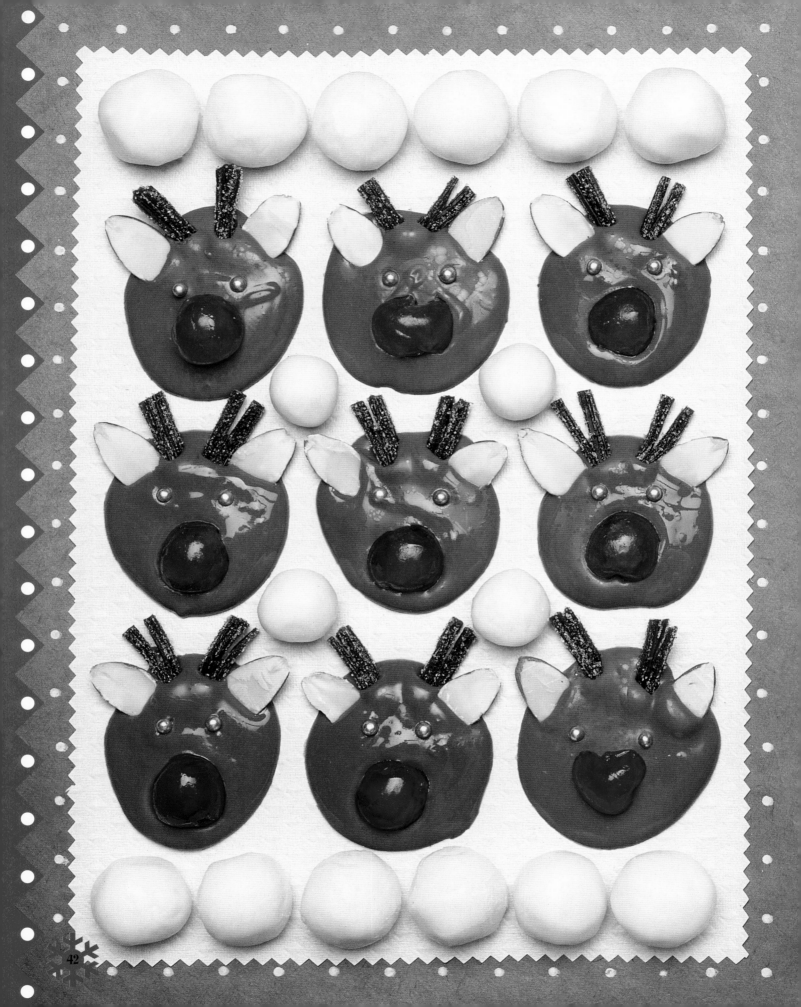

Sweets and treats

Tuck into minty snowballs and Rudolph chocolates all laid out on a plate, or wrap them up sweetly to give away as tasty gifts . . . yum yum!

Chocolate Rudolphs

You will need:

HALF ALMONDS

GLACÉ CHERRIES HALVED

JELLY STRIPS

SILVER BALLS

CHOCOLATE 170 G (6 OZ)

TRAY AND GREASEPROOF PAPER

Minty snowballs

You will need:

PEPPERMINT ESSENCE

ONE EGG WHITE

340 G (12 OZ) ICING SUGAR

TRAY AND GREASEPROOF PAPER

Making sweet treats

Chocolate Rudolphs

Melt the chocolate over a bowl of hot water.

Fill the bowl with boiling water.

Ask an adult to help with the hot water.

Spoon out dollops of chocolate.

Before the chocolate sets, add Rudolph's face.

Leave them to set.

Minty snowballs

Separate an egg.

Place an eggcup over the yolk.

Press the eggcup down firmly in place

Pour the white into another bowl.

Whisk up the egg white.

Stop whisking before the egg white gets too stiff.

Add four teaspoons of peppermint.

Add the egg white to the sugar.

Mix it all together.

Make into a ball.

The snowballs will be the size of large marbles.

Leave them to harden overnight.

Cut up the ball.

Make some snowballs.

Make some gifts

Use the projects in the book to create presents for your family and friends.

....Up, up, and away

Chilly treats

These secret pots can hold whatever you want. Keep the snowman and bring him out year after year.

Pop your biscuits into an air-tight biscuit tin and they will last a few weeks longer.

Gifts to eat

Decorate a biscuit tin and fill it with your spicy stars • A felt stocking can be filled with goodies and hung on the tree • Wrap up some minty snowballs in a cellophane bundle • Fill the snowmen with anything you want to give away

Leave the top of the sock open...

Festive fortune

Pot pourri will keep its scent if locked in a jar until it's time to give it away.

Fill woolies with dried lavender and sew up as shown on page 29.

You could fill a plastic bag with your mints.

Minty bundle

Gather it up at the top and tie with a ribbon.

Scented gifts

Decorate a jar of pot pourri with a bright, festive ribbon • Present pomanders in pretty boxes plumped up with tissue or material and finished off with a ribbon • Stuff your felt shapes with dried lavender for a scented decoration

Pretty pomander sits in a posh box.

Remember, the more cloves you use the longer your pomanders will last.

How to make pompoms and snowflakes

Woolly pompom

Make some pompoms to go with your winter woolies on page 28.

1 Cut two discs from thin card.

10 cm (4 in)

Cut a 3 cm- (1 ⅛ in-) diameter hole in the middle.

2 Put the two discs of card together.

Knot the wool in place.

3 Wind the wool around the discs.

Wrap the wool through the hole and around the disc.

Add more wool to completely cover the discs.

4 Put the scissors between the two discs.

Hold it firmly in the middle.

Snip the wool all the way round.

5 Open up the disc slightly.

Tie a piece of wool tightly around the middle.

Pull the card out and fluff up the wool.

6 Snip away any long bits to make a neat ball.

Make a square

To start off your paper snowflake it's handy to know how to make a square piece of paper.

Take a rectangular piece of paper.

Fold the top edge and line it up with one of the sides.

Cut off this piece.

Open it out and now you have a square shape.

Paper snowflakes

Paper snowflakes can be used in so many ways. Cut small ones to stick on greetings cards (page 4), medium-sized ones for festive windows (page 24), and really big ones to hang up as your bunting (page 12).

1 Take a piece of square paper of any size.

Fold the paper in half.

2 Fold it in half again...

3 ...and again.

4 Now start your design.

5 Draw on shapes.

6 Cut out the shapes.

7 Open it up.

Let's see what you've got.

All sorts of flakes

Woolly templates

Use these templates to make the winter woolies on pages 26-29.

Index

Acknowledgements

With thanks to...
Billy Bull, James Bull,
Seriya Ezigwe,
Daniel Ceccarelli, Lulu Coulter,
Harry Holmstoel for being
merry models.

All images © Dorling
Kindersley.
For further information see:
www.dkimages.com